THIS IS MY STORY

DENISE Y. TAYLOR-SMITH

Published by Denise Y. Taylor-Smith

ISBN 978-0-578-17102-9

Copyright 2015 All Rights Reserved

TABLE OF CONTENTS

Chapter	Title	Page
1	This Is My Story	9
2	My Grandmother	17
3	When Butterflies Filled the Air	20
4	Divorce	22
5	Dedra Is That You?	24
6	Precious Seed Of Life	27
7	For My Eyes Only	28
8	Yes	30
9	1976 The Bicentennial Year	34
10	July 8, 1981	37
11	Thanks Joe!	41
12	The Flip Side	43
13	A Tribute To Trayvon Martin's Mother	46
14	Single Life	47
15	There Is Something Left!	49
16	The Dream	53
17	My Prayer	54
18	Salvation Is Available Now!	57
19	Some Very Important Steps	59
20	The Sinner's Prayer	61
21	I Won't Bite	62
22	Our Lives Transition	64
23	April 17, 1993	66
24	My Children	73
25	A Mother's Crying Heart	75
26	Marriage	78
27	Crisis Averted!	83
28	Marriage Has Seasons	84
29	The Conversion Of King Twigg	89
30	My Husband	90

TABLE OF CONTENTS (CONTINUED)

Chapter	Title	Page
31	How We Keep Our Marriage Spicy	93
32	Live Your Days Aspired Anew	99
33	Praise Of A Virtuous Woman	101
	Acknowledgements	102
		103
		104
	Dedications	105
	More Words From The Author	106

Foreword

THIS IS MY STORY

By

Denise Y. Taylor-Smith

Some of the words written herein, are not necessarily grammatically correct. However, the chosen vernacular is for the purpose of capturing the essence of the moment.

Although some people in my story are now deceased, there are family members whom are still living. Some names are fictitious or not used at all as to not needlessly expose or embarrass any one.

CHAPTER 1 - THIS IS MY STORY

Who am I? I recently turned 62 and this question rises even more prominently in my soul than ever. Of course there is the obvious. I am a Christian (a follower of Christ), a wife of a successful man in his own right, a mother of a son 33, a daughter 22, a grandmother of four, a daughter from two deceased parents, a sister, a friend, a novice singer, a minister in our church... I didn't place an "and" on the last list item, because there are more sub categories of my life. But even with that listing there is a void, an unfulfilled journey, an opportunity missed, a decision never made, a place and a moment in time where I never really introduced myself to me. Yet still there is a glimmer of hope in what could be if I only dare try. It has been said that if you are not dead, then it is not too late and if you can believe it, you can conceive it. So here I am attempting to reveal, define and create me in a way that I have never done before, through writing. So when I am finished, I will add writer to my list along with an even more defined view of who I am. Fair? It is said that we are shaped by our experiences. Having said that, I feel we are also equally shaped by the experiences we didn't have. We live in a time where we are saturated with every source of immediate media gratification and reading has been deduced to Facebook, Tweeting, Instagram and the like. I'm guilty. I don't read books usually for entertainment. However, I do read for the purpose of gaining knowledge. I read the Bible. What I plan to share in this book may raise eyebrows for some. Before you judge me, finish reading my story and step back and look at your own life. I am writing my bio for self-clarification, for self-healing and to help someone else on this journey that we all share called life. So welcome, this is my story.

I was born in 1953 in a small, steel industry town which is classified as a 3rd class city. My mother started working at the Veterans Administration Hospital right out of high school, where she would continue working for forty five years. She was born in Wilson, North Carolina and she moved to Pennsylvania with her family when she was nine. My father was born in Philadelphia, I think. My mother and father were married for twelve years.

That's me in the middle!

My father had various jobs. The one I remember most vividly was a janitor job at the Presbyterian Church. He was also the pastor of a black Baptist church with a good sized congregation. My mom was our financial stabilizer. She was a good homemaker, wife and mother. She also was an excellent seamstress. She made most of her clothes, as well as mine. She sewed for some of the doctors and nurses she worked with, to pick up extra money. She also could sing. She had a beautiful voice and she sang on the church choir and around the house.

Mom and Me

Mom and Dad

My parents were gifted. I remember often asking my mom why she didn't become a singer. My dad was an excellent preacher. He could deliver a mighty word, but when it came to living it, he fell way short. From outside appearances we probably looked like an ideal family. My father had dreams that were never realized. I remember my mother would call him a pipe dreamer. She said this, meaning he talked a good game, but there was no action anywhere in sight to back up the words that came out of his mouth. My father was a womanizer. There were a lot of arguments. My mother cried a lot. She would do the laundry and find lipstick on his collar. Sometimes he would come home after being gone all weekend long, in time enough to get in the pulpit Sunday morning to preach. I remember one particular weekend we were going away with friends and my dad never came home. Such a let-down that was. I probably was about nine. I remember my dad lying in my bed because he was kicked out of his own and I would sit in the chair in the corner of my room asking my dad, "Why?" I was trying to get some understanding for his behavior by asking him, "Aren't you ashamed?" I was such a big girl. I shouldered a lot of responsibility to be so young. He used night school as an excuse to not be home in the evenings. He even introduced my sister and I to his woman as "Aunt So And So" (keeping her name anonymous), so that when we addressed her, we would automatically call her Aunt. Oh by the way, she too was married. Her husband thought my father and his wife were brother and sister (smdh). I could go on and on, but I will refrain, because my intent is not to bash my dad. However, these are some of the things that shaped me be it positive or negative. I also am aware that there are stories far worse than mine. But this is my story. My father had five other children, two before he married my mom, one from "Aunt So and So" and two others from two other marriages. Two of my siblings I don't know.

I had two other siblings, a brother and a sister, from my mother and father. My brother died of pneumonia when he was a baby. I loved my little sister. I took care of her frequently as my mother had to work. I would bathe her, dress her and comb her hair and anything else my mother needed me to do. When my sister died, my mother asked me if she loved her, as she probably could see in a way, a greater motherly bond between my sister and I, than the one between she and my sister. On the weekends, I would go to the movies downtown and I always had to take my little sister. I hated that. My friends would always say "Why you got to take her everywhere you go?" I don't know if this was my mother's way of keeping me out of trouble or just getting us both out of her way. Her nerves were always a wreck. Sometimes we, my mom, my sister and I would go visit her sister. I remember looking at my mom's face while she was driving. She looked so sad, which I remember clearly always gave me a feeling of such loneliness and helplessness. I didn't necessarily like this trip for that reason. My aunt's husband drank, a lot and one of my cousins was a tomboy. She took great pleasure in punching me in the arms. The other cousin was always trying to get me alone to do unmentionables. However, I always managed to get away from him. It was like a game, kinda fun, kinda scary. I was young and in my innocence. I didn't really know what I was dealing with.

Mom and Dad

My dad eventually abandoned us. I was twelve. My grandfather of whom I had no relationship with as his granddaughter, came and picked him up. I'll never forget that day. It was shocking. My dad didn't even say, "Goodbye" to me. My mother said, "What man would help his son leave his family?" She told him (my grandfather), that he would die like a dirty dog. He did, from a terminal illness. So now, it is the three of us which was a familiar feeling anyway, minus the arguing and fighting. Financially, it was a little tough for my mom. I remember having to wear a pair of boot styled shoes that were originally my mom's. I wore them until they were so run over! I thought I would never get a new pair of shoes! I felt even more embarrassed for my little sister. I remember watching my sister from across the street, at her bus stop while I waited at my bus stop for school. She had grown so much. She was tall and skinny and her dresses were now short and ridiculously small.

That's my sister Dedra on the left.

This Is My Story

My baby sis!

CHAPTER 2

MY GRANDMOTHER

    I had a great-grandmother. She was my father's, father's mother. I have said often, what my mother couldn't buy us she did. I said that because she said yes way more than she said no. Often times she would have me come and dust her furniture, and then she would give me the money. I remember a lot of weekends calling her up for money. For nostalgic purposes, let me describe this. I would go up a short flight of steps, lean over a wide, painted, wooden banister on the left and there hung a green phone on the wall. It is funny now with all of our technology, to think about being held hostage by a phone on the wall at the top of the first flight of stairs.

    I didn't have many friends and the kids always made fun of me. I was shy, very introverted and light skinned, so a lot of the kids took great pleasure in calling me white patty and they always wanted to beat me up. My grand mom was always there for me. When my bus arrived from school, my grand mom would walk across her backyard to meet me at the bus stop. She would have a look on her face that said, "I dare you to touch her!" She lived in her house down the street from us until she was 98. One day she had fallen in her bathtub. My uncle, my dad's brother, had her put into a nursing home for her safety as it was no longer safe for her to stay in her house. My grand mom died at the age of 114. I often wondered why the Lord had her hang on so long. One day I went to the nursing home to see her. I took her outside and wheeled her around the grounds. It was a warm, beautiful, sunny day. My grand mom said to me, "I don't know who you are, but you sure are a nice lady." That warmed my heart that day in an indescribable way. Before I started driving, my mom would take us. I could tell it was a trip she didn't enjoy. She would always say to me, when the time comes, please don't put me here. I must say it was a very gloomy, dingy, old looking facility on the inside. Outside it was a round large institutional building.

My grand mom's husband had died many years before I was born, but she didn't live alone. Her nephew lived with her. He was a drunk. I remember playing in the neighborhood. Back then it was real community. You knew your neighbors and just about everybody on the other streets. There were three that went around each other in a circle. There was one really poor family in the neighborhood. The father had walked out on his wife and two kids. She didn't work. My mom and dad went around the community and gathered food for them. Fathers worked, mothers kept house and worked, and children played outside until it was time for dinner in those days. I remember my mom calling me when it was time to come home. She would scream at the top of her lungs, because I could have been anywhere in the neighborhood, in a sing songy way, "NEEECIE!" So embarrassing!!! The kids would mock and make fun of me by repeating the cry, "NEEECIE!" I would drop whatever I was doing and run home. One, I knew it was dinner time. Two, in those days when you were called, you responded, or you got that tail whupped. After dinner, we had to stay on our street. When the street lights came on, we had better been in front of the front door. My grand mom used to stand bent over with her arms resting on the window seal, looking out her top floor window for hours. I used to love to look up when I was outside playing around her house and see her there. It was so reassuring!

I would visit my grand mom often and just sit at the kitchen table with her. There was only one issue. She never had any tasty treats! She was always offering me some rhubarb pie or some hard nasty cookies that she liked. Sometimes, when I would go to see her, she was watching her stories, General Hospital, As the World Turns, or One Life to Live. She had a huge, boxy, floor model, black and white TV which sat on four legs. My grand mom heated her house with coal. I guess we all did back then. These houses we lived in were old war tract houses.

They had rooms adjacent to the kitchen, beside the front door, that were called furnace rooms. The truck would come and deliver coal. The coal would slide down a shoot off the truck into a small square window right into the furnace room.

Remember the coal delivery man?

CHAPTER 3

WHEN BUTTERFLIES FILLED THE AIR

I can remember the warm, sunny beautiful days when butterflies filled the air. I would chase them for hours. My sister and I used to pick the blackberries from the bushes and eat them. Afterwards, I would pick the ticks off of her. There was no Lyme's Disease in those days. That was one of my favorite things to do, picking ticks off my sister and our neighbor's dog. The ways of a child! Every Saturday afternoon in the summer about midday, my sister and I would go in the house and take a bath for dress up day. My mom took great pride in dressing us up and doing our hair. I had a long fake ponytail. My mom would put my hair in a big bun with a chignon and stick the ponytail in the middle of it. Then I would go off to see my grand mom, walking in a way that would sway my ponytail back and forth, so she could see how cute I was.

Often times when I would go to see my grand mom, her nephew, cousin Floyd as I will call him, would not be there. "He's off somewhere gettin drunk!" my grand mom would say. There were times however, that he would be there. At times, he would be sober. When he was there and drunk, he would be talkin this high pitch gibberish that would make my grand mom say "Go on somewhere, Floyd!" When he was there and sober, he was quiet, down beat and dark. What my grand mom didn't know, was not only was he a drunkard, but, he was a pedophile. There were times my grand mom would go to the corner store and leave me at the house with him, when he was sober of course. I probably would have stood a better chance with him drunk. I was about nine years old.

(Note: The following account is graphically detailed.)

He took my hand after she had left and led me up the stairs. He took me in his room and shut the door, laid me on his bed, pulled up my dress, pulled down my panties and spread my legs open. He would stroke me until he was able to get it in. Then he humped me feverishly for a few moments, then it was over.

Looking back at that little girl laying there, it was no different than if he had screwed an infant! When it was over, he would say, "Get up and pull your panties up and go downstairs!" He would go into the bathroom. Usually I would go downstairs as he demanded. But one time I remember, I knocked on the bathroom door because I wanted to see this thing he was poking me with. He opened the door and slapped my face. Boy, that was confusing!

My grand mom came through the door with ice cream. She asked, "Where's Floyd?" Shrugging my shoulders, I said, "Upstairs." Imagine that! She could keep me safe from the bad ass kids in the neighborhood that wanted to beat me up. But she couldn't keep me safe from the old ass, musty smelling drunk pedophile!

But the Lord would heal my heart and my life from this tragedy. How many young girls bear this same burden alone in silence???

CHAPTER 4

DIVORCE

One morning I was in my mother's bedroom and she was listening to the radio. I remember hearing the word divorce. I asked my mother what that meant. She explained, that when two people don't love each other anymore, they decide not to stay married. This was a word I would be hearing again soon. It is funny how the mind works. There is the conscious and then there is the subconscious. When you're young, you're not aware of a subconscious mind until something triggers it. For me, it was the word divorce. One morning, my mom came in my room as I was making my bed and said, "Your father and I are getting a divorce." In that moment I felt like my whole world was coming apart. Even though, my dad had been gone awhile now, I had hoped that he would return. I didn't realize that he was never returning, until that moment.

It is not right for a child's childhood and innocence to be interrupted with abuse, harsh vulgarities, conscious self-seeking and selfish stops of love between those who said, "I do, until death do we part." Because in the middle of all of that, are children that are left alone, while you are fighting your war; leaving behind broken pieces, that will need to be ever so delicately put back together. Who can reassemble a damaged child? I felt like trash strewn about that needed to be gathered before the wind blew me away. The things I had experienced up until that point were enough to impact me in a most negative way for some time to come.

My mother was beautiful, and her positive furor, drove her past her pain. She had no shortage of male attention. They came, and they went. One stayed awhile. When he was sober, he was the nicest guy you ever would want to meet. When he was drunk, he was somebody different. I would hear the enraged, jealous arguments behind my bedroom door. He even threatened to kill my mom by throwing her out of the window. Then in the light of day the sobbing, begging and the I'm "sorries" would fill the air.

Eventually, my mom gets rid of him and she meets someone else. He's older, a widower and had his own business. He was financially stable. He had a big house and drove a brand new Lincoln Continental. They dated for a little while and my mom seemed happy. After a short courtship, they married. We moved into his big house. We felt like we had struck it rich. He bought my mom a brand new Cadillac and she was able to keep her pay check for herself. My mom redecorated the house with paint and new furniture. We were livin good until my mom decided that it was not quite what she wanted. The things were great, but that would not hold her marriage together. They managed to stay together for six years. During those six years there were affairs on both sides. There were more arguments. I never spoke a word to my stepfather other than those that were necessary, nor did he speak to me. I felt like a doll that was placed in a doll house.

CHAPTER 5

DEDRA IS THAT YOU?

My sister and I shared a bedroom. We had twin beds, pink walls, frilly curtains and bedspreads and pretty girly, white French provincial furniture and a big Tabby cat named Tippy. He slept on my sister's bed. One afternoon, I was down in the family room on the phone, talking to my boyfriend. I was sixteen, my sister was seven. The night before, my sister had spent the night with her little girlfriend who lived across the highway. Our house sat back off of the highway and we had a good sized front yard with a fence, but the house sat on a highway. I was on the phone, and my mom was in the kitchen cooking dinner. I heard my sister asking my mom could she go back to her friend's house, because she forgot her pajamas. I heard my mom say, "You can go after dinner." Just moments after she said that I heard the front door open and shut. What I heard next made me drop the phone and run outside. There I saw my sister lying stretched out in the highway. Her one leg was crossed over the other and her shoes were off and scattered in the highway. My mother was screaming and the man was saying, "She just ran out in front of me!" It was so surreal. My stepsister was home from law school at that time. The next thing that I remember clearly, was she and I walking into the emergency ward at the Coatesville Hospital. As we walked up the walkway, there was wailing by my mother who was already there because she rode in the ambulance. My stepsister had her arm around me and she squeezed me tightly and she said "The Lord giveth and the Lord taketh away." My little sister had passed. The doctor said she didn't suffer, because the impact killed her instantly. My God! What a sad day! And many more sad days followed, as people from the church and the community came by to express their condolences. I remember feeling numb for a long time! I guess numb was good.

*"One night I was awakened by Tippy moving around on her bed.
"Dedra, is that you?" I asked.
When I realized it was the cat and my sister was gone, I cried the rest of the night until the sun came up.
My face and eyes were swollen in such a way that I would never see my face look that way again."*

IN LOVING MEMORY OF

DEDRA PAULINE TAYLOR

Born: October 6, 1959

In the Lord's Embrace : August 3, 1967

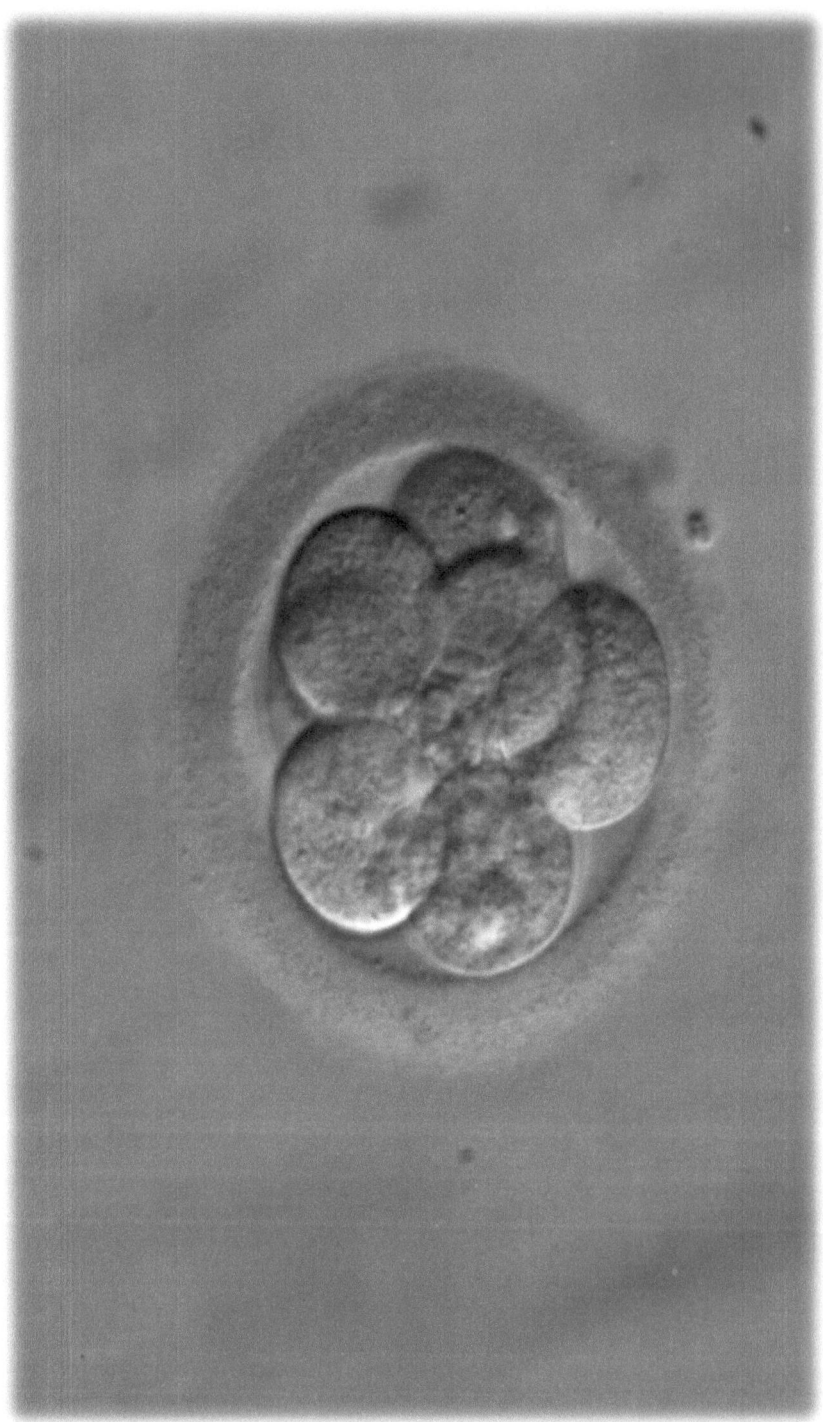

CHAPTER 6

PRECIOUS SEED OF LIFE

I had become sexually active by my own volition two weeks before my sixteenth birthday. Soon, I became pregnant. My mother found out by listening in on my phone call with my boyfriend. "You need to tell your mom that you are pregnant", he said. " Yesss!" she screamed in the phone, "You need to tell me!" Getting pregnant out of wedlock back then was shameful and embarrassing. So my mother ran the gamut from angry and fussing me out, to angry and not talking to me. Finally, she softened and would hold me while I cried, "Mommy I'm not a bad girl!" I guess she also got relief from the embarrassment of the situation too, because my stepsister who lived in Washington, DC told her about a doctor who performed abortions. My mother, stepfather and I proceed to leave, ten o'clock at night getting into the car in the garage and headed to Washington. We arrived at this doctor's office in the wee hours of the morning. I never had a say in this at all. I didn't have a chance to think or feel anything but shame. I laid back on a hard cold steel table, with a bright light over me magnifying my shame. He put a tube inside of me and poured a solution down the tube which felt cold and sterile. A few hours later there was hard cramping, and then, I passed the baby I would never hold, see, smell or speak to lovingly. So set the precedent for more abortions. I used birth control pills for a while, but when I felt they weren't healthy for me to continue to take, abortion was always an option.

Much time has passed since those days. I want to make it clear that in no way am I pro abortion! The life that God plants in a womb is not a mistake! The act itself might not be of God, but the seed is never a mistake. Life and death is God's business. Last I checked, He IS the greatest I AM and He holds all things in his hands!

CHAPTER 7

FOR MY EYES ONLY

I had a close friend. Her mother and my mother were close friends. My mom would take me and my friend on vacation to Atlantic City where we stayed at the Traymore Hotel. It was very ritzy! We loved it, because whatever rules there were to follow we totally abandoned them there. My mother was partying. She wasn't keeping her eye on us. But she tried. Please, really??? We would go down on Atlantic Avenue to Club Harlem. We couldn't get in, but the music was loud and the jazz filled the air. The atmosphere was electric with excitement and a good time. My friend and I looked older than we were. Add that in with purvey guys and that made for a dangerous mix to our detriment. We ended up in a car with two guys. They were handsome and suited and jerks! They drove us someplace where we didn't know where we were. Then they started talking back in forth to each other as to what they were going to do to us. I was sitting in the front next to the driver. My friend was sitting in the back with his friend. Then the guy driving, leaned over and opened up the glove box which displayed a gun. I was scared to death! They pulled over on this vacant street. In an instant, without hesitation, my girlfriend and I both jumped out the car at the same time and started running. We didn't know where we were, but we knew we were getting away from there! After we felt sufficiently out of sight, we walked and walked, vowing we would never do something like that again. God truly protected us! We did eventually find our way back to the hotel. We went quickly to our room and got in the bed, where we should have been in the first place. We were both very thankful to be back where we belonged that night!

The night before we left on this trip to Atlantic City, my girlfriend spent the night and she was sleeping in my sister's bed. I laid across the bottom, as I did so many nights before because it was right against a window. I used to love to lay there and look out at the stars. This night, I would see more than stars. It was a clear, beautiful, star filled summer night. There appeared so quickly, seemingly coming out of nowhere, a huge, oval shape with lights all around it. It hovered over the highway. The outside was spinning and the inside was still. It hovered there for a moment and then glided off, disappearing just as quickly as it showed up. "Chloe! Chloe! Look, look! Get up, you got to see this!" I said. "Whatever it is, I don't want to see", she said. There I was seeing something so amazing, something I never imagined I would ever see. Oh well, for my eyes only, I guess. I have not forgotten it until this very day!

CHAPTER 8

YES

My mother and stepfather managed to stay together until I graduated from high school and subsequently flunked out of college after just one year. After that, I guess my mother didn't see any reason to keep hanging on. She had a boyfriend that was several years younger than her. She came to me and said, "I'm leaving and you have to find somewhere to go." So I did. I had started seeing someone who was married. But he told me he was separated. I believed him of course. But by the time I found out the truth, I loved him and didn't care. I told him I had to find a place to live, because my mom doesn't want me around her young boyfriend. He got an apartment. We bought furniture and started our lives together. He was twenty six and I was nineteen and dumb. He drove a tractor trailer, when he felt like it. The rest of his time was spent in illegal pursuits. Things were good for a while. He introduced me to the bars and drinking and he also confirmed my hunch that men are "dirty dogs!" He came in the apartment one day; I was sitting on the floor at the foot of the bed watching TV. He asked me to marry him and gave me this little a** diamond ring. I remember handing it back to him and saying, "I don't want to get married!" I knew I would get married one day, but it wasn't going to be to a lying, cheating drug dealer. I guess I wasn't so dumb after all. With that rejection, he amped up his cheating ways. But before this relationship was through, I would experience having the SWAT team bust in our apartment door, while I was not dressed, tear up the apartment by throwing things around, dropping the food in the refrigerator on the floor, having a police officer watch me while I put my clothes on, and then being made to sit in a chair and told not to move. We had beautiful furniture and two large fifty five gallon fish tanks with salt water fish in the top tank and two large Oscars in the bottom.

The police were sizing us up and commenting on how much drug money he was making because of the stuff they saw. It was so freaking humiliating! But they didn't find anything. However, that wasn't my last encounter with law enforcement.

I did end up in jail on another occasion because of his illegal activities. After dropping him off at a particular location in Lancaster, I started my return home. It had started snowing really hard, so hard that I ended up pulling over because it was coming down so aggressively, that the conditions were a white out. Little did I know that the police were following me. The lights started flashing in back of me. I proceeded to get out when I heard a loud voice saying, "Get back in the car!" After waiting a few moments, I was ordered to get out of the car with my hands up. I was pushed against the car, patted down, handcuffed and then shoved into the back of a police car (Aggressive policing has been around for quite awhile!). Off the officer drove, while another recited my Miranda rights. "You have the right to remain silent. Anything you say or do may be used against you in a court of law. You have the right to an attorney. If you cannot afford one, one will be appointed to you by a court of law. Do you understand what I just said?" "Yes", I replied. I didn't know where they were taking me. But by morning, I was in a Harrisburg prison.

I was out shopping with my mom one day. I was in the eleventh grade and the shag hairdo was popular at that time. We came across this sharp shag wig. My mom said, " Try it on!" We loved it. I looked so good in this wig. My mom bought it and that was the beginning of a lifetime of wearing wigs. I braided up my fro and became more in touch with my "other" side just by changing my hair.

When I arrived at the prison, I had to strip, remove my wig, shower and wash my hair with this harsh stinky soap in front of a woman officer. After that, she threw this powder on me. With my beautiful, long, locks removed, I have this tight, dried- out, nappy head of uncomb-able hair. Not even any products to make my fro beautiful! Then, I was locked up in this small, dank cell with a toilet with no seat. I was in there long enough to have 3 meals, which I didn't eat, be put in a larger room which had a tiny TV on the wall up high in the corner. I sat in the corner by myself quietly while I observed the women talk about me like they were guys. The humiliation I was experiencing knew no boundaries!

My mother and a friend of my mother, whom was a bail bondsman, came to our rescue. You see, my boyfriend had been picked up as well. Later it was said, that which saved me from being prosecuted was the fact I didn't turn around and go back to Lancaster to pick him up. So, my story of not knowing what was going on; and I was just dropping him off, held up.

CHAPTER 9

1976 THE BICENTENNIAL YEAR

If I had only caught a clue, then 1976, the bicentennial year wouldn't have been so memorable. We, my boyfriend and I were on our way to Atlantic City for the weekend. We were in the apartment getting ready to leave. "I'll be right back. I'm going to take the bags to the car." The next thing I knew he was coming back into the apartment with his hands in the air and two males in back of him, one with a gun in his back! They ordered us to sit down. We did, at the table. They were asking him, "Where is the money! Where are the drugs???" He kept saying he didn't know what they were talking about. I pleaded with him to give them what they wanted. He even had the nerve to get smart with the guy who had the gun in his face, saying, "F***k you man!!" Those proved to be my boyfriend's last words. The guy proceeded to hit him with the butt of the gun across his temple. The assailants were desperate and things quickly escalated. No sooner than he hit him, he shot him point blank, in the fore head. I saw his tongue roll out as he fell back. The other guy shot me. The sound of the gun going off made me duck. The bullet hit me in the top of my head. I was still conscious, with my head leaned over the table. My boyfriend's son who was seven, had spent the night and we were going to drop him off at home on the way. This young child saw everything!! They ordered the child and I, to get down on the floor. Then they tied us up with phone cord they had pulled out of the wall. I laid there with my face in the carpet as they resumed asking me about money and drugs. I couldn't tell them because I didn't know the whereabouts of his stash. They cleaned out my boyfriend's pockets as I laid there thinking about my mother viewing my body in a casket.

I just knew they were going to shoot me again. One said to the other "Let's get out of here!" and they left. I laid there with my heart pounding and I was too afraid to move. I waited to hear a car leave, but it didn't happen. So I summoned the strength to pull my hands free and then freed my boyfriend's son.

I looked out of the peep hole in the door. I didn't see anyone, so I open the door slowly and peeked out. Then I grabbed his hand and ran like hell, with blood running down my face, to the apartments three buildings over, to my girlfriend and her husband's place. She answered the door, with her baby in her arms. She had a look of horror on her face as she viewed us standing there. This was not a typical day for she nor I. She called the ambulance to our apartment for my boyfriend and she took me to the hospital.

As they worked on me, the doctor said, "This is one lucky young lady!" The bullet had entered in at the top of my head and blew out the back of my head without penetrating my skull. I was in the hospital for a week for observation. My boyfriend wasn't so fortunate. He died at the end of the week after being on life support. I never went back to the apartment. When I was in the hospital, there was a night when there was a bad thunderstorm and someone had broken into the apartment by smashing the sliding glass doors. They helped themselves to TVs, jewelry and whatever else they wanted. My dad had given me a beautiful pearl and diamond ring. I never wore it, because I felt it was a little mature for me at that time, but it was beautiful and my dad gave it to me and now it was gone!

After this tragic event, I moved in with my mom until I left to go to Altadena, California, where my dad had lived. I was totally paranoid. Every car that pull up or passed by my mom's apartment sent me reeling, peeking out of the window. My heart was gripped with fear.

When I arrived on the west coast, to live with my dad, it wasn't any better even though I was now separated by the width of the continent, from the physical location of my victimization. The bedroom I slept in had windows from the ceiling to the floor, with all sorts of large leaf plants on the outside, which was for privacy instead of curtains. I always felt like they were coming for me. They hadn't been caught yet. I spent much time pouring over sketches and pictures that the detectives brought me to review. The sketches were created from the description I gave them, when I was in the hospital. I spent a year flying back and forth, from the west coast to the east coast, going to court after they were caught. It was finally over. They both received a good amount of time. Also, my boyfriend's cousin was tried and convicted on conspiracy charges, because she set the whole thing up and drove them to our apartment. That gave me some relief, but I didn't get back to normal living for quite some time. I stayed on the east coast for several unproductive years, marked with several "in and out" relationships, until I finally went back to California.

CHAPTER 10

July 8, 1981

    While I was in California, I got pregnant. Then I married the father of my unborn baby, on February 14, 1981. We had our son on July 8, 1981. I was 28. What a joyous day. He was beautiful. He was such a sweet baby. Every time I smiled at him, he would smile right back with this large, bright smile. I was his mommy and he was my son. I loved him then and I love him now. His father and I had only been married for a short while. but it was evident we weren't going to last. He had heavy mood swings. I was battling with my own depression. I saw this before I married him, but I wanted to believe it would be okay when we got married. We were together two years, before we separated, never to reunite, until we finally divorced, 11 years later. One evening, as he slept on the couch, I packed up everything I could in the suit cases that were under the bed. I stripped the bed and put clothing items and baby things in the bed sheets and pillow cases. What prompted this sudden move? I over heard my husband the night before on the phone talking about he was sending our son to Louisiana to stay with his sister. He loved playing head games with me, abuse in a different way. I was not waiting around to see if this was true. I had enough. I drove from Anaheim to Palm Springs, to where my dad had moved. I had never been there. That was pretty amazing. I drove in the dark of early morning, about 95 miles through the desert, alone with my baby. There was nothing in sight for miles and miles except huge oil rigs. I made one stop at a restaurant to call my dad to let him know I was on my way. I had my baby in my arms and when I got back to the car I realized he had lost his passey (pacifier). Good thing he was a good baby. I left the apartment about 5AM and pulled up at my dad's house about 7AM. What a relief! That was quite a trip for me and my 16 month old baby. My dad and his family were kool with us being there. We stayed for a little while, about a month, then I decided to move back to the east coast to be close to my mom.

After arriving back to the east coast, we lived with my mom for a while, because at this point, she lived alone. She loved her grandson. I found a job and decided to get my own place. Now, my mother didn't want me to go. The place where I moved was subsidized, meaning your rent is according to your income. The apartments were nice for me and my son. As for my mom, she let me know I was moving to the Ghetto. Ghetto or not, I was going to have my own place where my son could have his own nicely decorated room and I could have my own space. My son and I had a new beginning in our new apartment. I bought new furniture, paintings and plants. My apartment was beautiful. There was a young girl who lived across the street from me who watched my son while I went to work as a sales rep for Levitt's Furniture. After discovering she wasn't caring for my son in the way I desired, I let my job go. I ran an ad to do housecleaning services and obtained more work than I could handle. I even got a contract with an apartment building. I was able to work while my son was in school and be home by the time he got home. I remember my son's first day of school, and putting him on the bus was traumatic for me. That was the first time we had ever been apart. In my mind's eye, I can see his cute little face looking back at me from the school bus window. When I realized his expression was mimicking my expression, I gave him a big smile, his face lit up with that huge familiar smile that he shared so easily. When I got back to the apartment I cried so hard. You would have thought I just sent my son away never to return. I loved and love my son!

Me and Baby Joey

My Son Joe

CHAPTER 11

THANK'S JOE!

In the days that followed, he made a lot of friends. He was a sweet, kind and outgoing kid. He and his friends would run in and out of the apartment. There was Jamir, Jon Jon, Talvin, Leon and Moo. When he was alone he would play by himself pretending like he was my puppy, down on his hands and knees, barking and rubbing his head on my legs. I would put a bowl of water down on the floor, where he would lap it up, wagging his body like a happy little puppy, then begging for more up on his knees, arms at his side, hands drooped down and tongue out panting. Then there were the times when he played with his trucks by lining them up from his bedroom to the living room. He would say, "Look mommy, it's a traffic jam!" I would smile and say, "I'm sure glad I'm not in that mess!" That boy had quite a few trucks and other toys and books, thanks to his dad, Joe. He sent support money, seasonal clothing and toys, which helped to make it easier for me to take good care of my son. Thanks Joe! You might think, why are you thanking somebody for doing what they are supposed to do? Well in a society where men drop their seed here and there with reckless abandonment, living their lives with no concern for their children's well-being emotionally, spiritually or financially, my hat is off to the ones who do care and take an active part in the lives of their children.

Easter Sunday circa 1983

CHAPTER 12

THE FLIP SIDE

The flip side of that, is women who choose to have children without a father in place, or women who choose to leave the father, as I did. These decisions are made often times with no real consideration of a future, but only the present moments at hand. Children can't do what's best for their lives. They can only depend on mommy and/or daddy, to transact that piece which often times, is miserably mishandled because we are busy trying to recoup that which has failed us in the relationship. For the most part, parents love their children. But sometimes that is not enough to guide them to a proper future. I believe key components are missing when both parents are not present. Of course, there are many scenarios which can obstruct this conducive environment, so this can not be a blanket statement but only an observation. However, as a two parent home, agreement between parents is key. As a blended family, agreement among parents is key. And for a single parent home, a more than an occasional "no" is imperative. If you don't set healthy barriers for your children they will not be prepared for nor able to overcome all of the "no's" that will come once they are no longer in your loving protective care. If you want your arms of love to wrap around your children long after they have left the home (assuming they have left) then give them clear, consistent discipline. That in and of itself, with love and guidance, will go a long way for making a strong, determined and responsible individual.

CHAPTER 13

A TRIBUTE TO TRAYVON MARTIN'S MOTHER

As I watched the events of the Trayvon Martin case unfold, the cold brevity of the situation moved my heart for his mother, Sybrina Fulton, in addition to my general concern for mothers who suffer for their sons. My second husband, whom I am married to now, while at work could actually sense that I was crying watching Ms. Fulton's plight over the loss of Trayvon. He penned these lyrics and arranged this song, A Nation of Mothers. I am actually singing my heart's sentiment to Ms. Fulton. The song can be found on YouTube.

https://www.youtube.com/watch?v=n9El5fAiEQc

"A Nation of Mothers" Thank you for viewing and listening.

A NATION OF MOTHERS

Copyright 2012, By Allen Smith

I remember when my son was a child,
How he used to hold on to my side,
Remembering his sweet precious laugh and smile,
Made every struggle to care for him worth the fight

Watching him sleep, watching him rest,
I knew God blessed me with him
That's how I know He blessed you with your son too..

I really feel your loss,
I really feel your pain,
Your wound can't be described,
Your tears flow from my eyes.
But we're a Nation of Mothers by your side.

"To all mothers who have suffered the loss of a son, to death, incarceration, or the misdirection of life, that our young minority men often take the path of, and their lives are still being stolen because of a society whom still view Black Lives as valueless, we are a "Nation of Mothers by your side!"

Me, Mom and Joey

CHAPTER 14

SINGLE LIFE

(So Many Beaus and All I Got Was Knots)

My new single life living in an apartment, raising my young son, was good for a while. I was dating, but, never meeting that so called "better half." I dated money. I dated the father of the founder of a popular group from back in the 1980's, "Take 6". I dated professionals and I even crossed the color line a time or two. The ones I wanted to stay didn't and the ones that wanted to stay I didn't want. Loneliness pervaded my soul like a wet blanket. I would sleep just to get away from that gnawing feeling of loneliness.

One thing I come to realize is that a woman is a responder to a man's love. Sometimes we are responding to what we hope is love. Ladies you do not have to work so hard and put out so much for the love of a man. To bounce back from a bad relationship can be hard and it can skew your view on men and relationships. To all my sisters old and young who are alone and don't want to be, God wants you to respond to his love first by faith. The pain of being alone can be more valuable than being stuck in a bad relationship. If your attitude is a bad relationship is better than no relationship, then you need to STOP and take an assessment of yourself. If you need help with this self evaluation, seek help. If you can pay for professional help, do it. If you can't afford it, seek people you can trust and you respect, e.g. parents, pastors, loyal friends, your local community battered woman's shelter... This world we live in is a mess and people are messed up. There seems to be no moral compass and certainly a Godly compass is hard to find. But, turn your gaze inward that is where you will find the source for every need and desire to be meant if the Holy Spirit is present.

It is not surprising that marriage is skewed and not popular anymore. As we move more into the age of the church falling away (2 Thessalonians 2:3) so goes marriage. For marriage mirrors Christ being married to the church, His bride (Ephesians 5:23-33). Marriage can't really be embraced by those whose minds are fixed on the temporary; I'm living for today, what can you do for me and what have you done for me lately?

Naomi had two daughter-in-laws. When her sons died, one daughter-in-law left to go back to her land and her gods. The other daughter-in-law, Ruth, said, "I will stay with you and serve your God!" It wasn't long before, Boaz saw her and immediately started making provision for her as she worked in the field. My point is, if you never settle yourself before the Lord and you keep receiving beaus? All you will get is knots. Knots take time to undue and your Boaz will always be an unfulfilled place in your heart. The pain of being alone while you wait on God is certainly a better use of your time if you take that time to prepare yourself. Every man encounter that you receive to yourself as a possible suitor will come with something you like, but will not necessarily address the desire and needs of the whole woman. Don't search for him, just prepare to be found.

I found a new job working in the treasurer's office at the court house. My mom's good friend, an elderly lady and her daughter took care of my son while I worked. My own mother was still working at the time.

CHAPTER 15

THERE IS SOMETHING LEFT!

One evening, a friend of mine called and asked me to go to a church revival service with her in Harrisburg. She lived in Lancaster. She said if I drove to her house, she would drive to Harrisburg. My friend was so excited. She talked about this young minister who was going forth in the word of God. She was saying people were getting healed, saved and delivered. Her enthusiastic appeal sparked my interest. Also having a young minister to sit and look at all evening was really exciting too! I told her if my baby sitter, Ms. Alice, didn't mind watching Joey for the evening, after he has been there all day, I would go. After work I go to Ms. Alice's house, and it just so happens she is having a party for one of her grand kids. Kids were everywhere, running around having fun. Joey wasn't ready to go. He was a kid's kid. Wherever there was fun, Joey was there! Ms. Alice standing on her porch assured me it was okay that he stayed. Joey without any warning jumped off her high stone wall right into my arms and gave me a big hug. That scared me and made me scream, " You sure are a trusting little boy!" "If he can't trust you, who can he trust?" said Ms. Alice. With many thank you's to Ms. Alice and hug and kisses to my baby, off I went. Child secure, check, Friday evening free, check and a place to go, check, check. I was feeling great! I called my friend and off I went. When I arrived at her house, we hugged, and jump into her car. I asked her if I was dressed okay? My dress was showing my curves, my heels made me look like a tall drink of water and my hair was flowing. After all we were going to church. She said I look great! Harrisburg here we come!

By the way, this is the friend who took me to the hospital when I was shot in the head about 8 years before. When we got there the church was full. People were praising the Lord and the minister was more than I expected. He was this silky chocolate smooth, curly headed brother in a clean, sharp white suite, silky white shirt and red tie with white shoes, uhmm, uhmm, uhmm. I'll go to church evvverry Sunday to look at that! This was truly a revival! We went in, sat down and the minister was pouring it on. Everyone around me was so excited. As for me, I wasn't moved at all, at least not buy the Holy Spirit. But what I was moved by was the change in my friend. The ride back to my friend's place was the longest ride ever. She had the nerve to ask me if I knew the Lord. I thought to myself as I gave a low screechy, "yes", who the hell do you think you are? I'm a PK. She went on and on talking about how she loved HIM and how HE loves us and how HE suffered and died for us so that we might live and live again. She went on to say how she used to think highly of herself. You see, she was red-bone too and beautiful. Her husband and my boyfriend who was killed, were best friends and he introduced me to them. She and her husband had met in college in the South. When they graduated, he brought her back North with him. She said when we were introduced, she thought to herself, "Oh no he didn't bring another pretty yellow b****h around and got the nerve to be nice!"

You see, my friend had changed. I was uncomfortable and that ride was long. I thought to myself here goes a friendship. I couldn't wait to get out of her car. Finally we arrive back at her place. It's late. We say our good byes and I take off. On my ride home my thoughts were racing. I don't really remember the ride as much as I remember how disturbed I was. When I got inside my apartment and shut the door, I fell apart. I felt so ashamed. I was no stranger to the Lord. My dad had been a pastor. I grew up in the church and I accepted Christ and was baptized when I was six. I knew the Lord and He knew me. What I had realized was "I got saved", but I never grew out of the infancy stage of my salvation. It is now two in the morning and I am weeping and dialing my changed friend up on the phone. "Hello", a deep, sleepy who the hell is callin this time of the mornin voice answered. "H**k (Her husband), it's Denise", "I know it's late, I'm sorry, but, can I please speak to J**y (My friend)?" There's silence. "Who is it?", asked J**y (In the back ground). "Denise", said H**k. "Hello", "J**y, help me!" "I'm so ashamed!" "I never grew out of the infancy stage of my salvation!" "I know you don't know everything, but will you at least help me to get where you are?" That morning until about three AM, J**y ministered to me and prayed for me. When I finally went to bed and laid my head on my pillow, it seemed like in that same instance, I was sound asleep. The next morning was Saturday. I was awakened in the most unusual way. My eyes popped open as though someone had called my name. Then I heard in an audible reassuring voice, "There is something left and I want it back!"

This Is My Story

CHAPTER 16

THE DREAM

Two weeks before this, I had a dream that was so disturbing it rocked me to my core. In my dream, I wanted to die! The dream was very explicit and vivid. In my dream, I stood in the street, in front of my apartment and poured gasoline on myself and lit a match. I was burning! I could feel the pain! My face was burning first. Only thing I wasn't dying. My neighbor who lived upstairs put the fire out and cradled me in her arms and rocked me back and forth. I was so upset and mad she didn't let me die. When I awoke from the dream I was so upset because I had such a strong will to die in the dream. I never thought about suicide or wanting to die. I loved life; or at least I thought I did. Several weeks had gone by and I had forgotten about the dream, but when the Lord awakens me on this morning and said, "There is something left and I want it back!", He revealed to me the meaning of the dream. He was saying I was sick with sin even unto death, but I had done nothing so wrong that He couldn't save me from it. He showed me it was Him that was cradling and rocking me in the street. In the blink of an eye, I was delivered and set free by the power of God. In the days that followed, they were nothing short of a miracle after miracle.

During the time when I worked at a popular furniture store, I worked with a bunch of guys (12) on the sales floor and 3 ladies, including myself. There was a lot of foul talking, and now my ears could not bear to hear it. I would go into the coat room and pray:

CHAPTER 17

MY PRAYER

"Dear Heavenly Father in the name of Jesus, thank you for forgiving me of my sins.

Thank you for loving me more than I loved myself. Show me how to please you.

Father there will be a huge void in my life if I stop all the sinful things that I do.

I don't want to drink anymore; I don't want to sleep around anymore,

I don't want to do any of the things that will cause you not to be pleased with me.

Help me Lord! I need you! Amen".

When I was done my prayer, He said to me in that audible voice, "Don't you worry about those things, just give your life over to me completely and I will take care of everything else!" I was so in love with my Lord. I was all a-glow. Everything had become new. One morning I stopped at Mickey D's to get my usual bacon and egg breakfast sandwich before going into work. I found I couldn't eat it. My taste had become so sensitive to grease. I threw it out. When I got to work and walked into the break room one of the guys who I never had a conversation with said, "Denise, come here." He was calling me to the kitchen. When I got there he handed me three beautiful roses and said, "These grow in my yard and I thought you would appreciate them." I was so surprised I couldn't contain my tears.

He was married and this was not a come on. It was pure and sincere. To me the three roses represented one for the Father, the Son and the Holy Ghost. My Heavenly Father delivered flowers to me. There was another guy I did talk to personally at the job. We had become friendly in our work environment. I shared all of my new found revelation and my growing personal relationship with my Lord with him. He was drawn by my testimony and the next day I got a beautiful card from him that said, "I asked Jesus how much do you love me?" And Jesus spread his arms and died for me. So many wonderful things happened that week. While I was out on the sales floor, I looked down at the palms of my hands and both my palms were bruised in the center. My God was showing out for me! He had already done His greatest act of love for the whole world, now He was being intimate with me.

On the weekend I went shopping in Philadelphia. I passed by a jewelry store where I had stopped to browse at the beautiful pieces. The diamonds and precious gems began to pale in comparison to the glory of my God! And as I continued to gaze at the precious gems, I was beginning to lose my high that I was on from falling in love with Jesus. As I walked on down the crowded street I saw a woman coming straight for me. She said, "Ma'am can you spare a nickel, quarter or a dime?" I felt moved to give her a dollar. She was so thankful. This was so amazing to me, because out of all the people on the street, she could have asked, she locked in on me.

This Is My Story

CHAPTER 18

SALVATION IS AVAILABLE NOW!

No matter what day to day living brings your way, whether it is good or bad, you can make changes where needed. You really can accept the things you cannot change; simply by leaving it in the hands of the Lord. And as for those things, God's outcome is never wrong. For you too, have a story and God has a plan just for you. Life can be tough. If you are shouldering your existence with your own strength, you have no idea just how much peace and satisfaction you can get from this existence called life. Truly, it can be more than existing, but truly living, if you turn your life over to God. Life is a story that continues day by day. It is filled with ups and downs. Sometimes the downs seem to outweigh the ups. It is said there are two things you can be sure of, death and taxes. As for your taxes, pay them. As for death? The price has been paid for you. If you would like to reserve your place in Heaven through Jesus Christ? Jesus says I am the way, the truth, and the life: no man cometh unto the Father, but by me (John 14:6). Romans 10: 13 says, "For whosoever shall call upon the name of the Lord shall be saved."

This Is My Story

CHAPTER 19

SOME VERY IMPORTANT STEPS

1) RECOGNIZE YOUR CONDITION. For all have sinned and come short of the glory of God (Romans 3:23). Just being a good person won't get you into Heaven.

2) REALIZE THE PENEALTY FOR YOUR SIN. For the wages of sin is death (Romans 6:23). When you don't except Jesus Christ as your personal savior then your sins are not forgiven and the penalty for your sin is eternal death in a place called Hell.

3) BELIEVE CHRIST DIED FOR YOU AND THAT HE LOVES YOU. "But God commendeth his love toward us, in that, while we were yet sinners, Christ died for us" (Romans 5:8). Christ gave up his life on the cross for the whole world, but all who receive him have personal access to love and salvation.

4) TRUST CHRIST ALONE AS YOUR SAVIOUR. For God so loved the world, that he gave his only begotten Son, that whosoever believeth in him should not perish, but have everlasting life (John 3:16). For whosoever shall call upon the name of the Lord shall be saved (Romans 10:13). Everlasting life is a gift purchased by the blood of Jesus Christ and offered freely to those who call upon Him by faith. If you want to know this God that I speak about then pray this prayer:

This Is My Story

CHAPTER 20

THE SINNER'S PRAYER

Dear Father, I realize that I am a sinner who is in need of a Saviour. I ask that you would come into my heart and save me from all of my sins. Help me to know more about you and I am putting all my trust in you and you alone. When I die I want to be with you in Heaven. Thank you for being my Saviour, thank you for being my Lord. In Jesus name, Amen!

CHAPTER 21

I WON'T BITE

One summer day in 1971, I was 18 and had just graduated high school, I was walking with my friend down the street to her house and this little boy about nine years old is playing with his little buddies. He is sitting on his two wheeler with his butterfly handle bars and banana seat. His friend says, "She is pretty!" referring to my girlfriend, and he says, "No, I think her friend is fine!" So he says to me, "Hey baby!" I was shocked at this young boy talking like that and immediately replied, "OOH! You fresh cuss!" To hear him tell it, he thought he was well with in his bounds making a pitch for a girl. Many years go by and this young man grows up and I see him working in a supermarket. I get in his line because he is fast. Later I would learn from him, he was slow but speeded up when he saw me so I would get in his line. He would always have something to say to me to let me know he was interested. I would be thinking "Go on young boy, you don't have nothing for me! You're too young and you're working in a grocery store!" But to his credit, he had just graduated college and he was always talking about the next better opportunity. At that time I did not know that the grocery store was his part time job, in part because he was always there. Which at that time, for where I was looking to be, this was a turn off. However, I did give him my number.

One day I was in the supermarket doing my grocery shopping, and as usual I get in Ty's line, because he is fast. Also, I have to tell you I don't recognize this guy as the little boy that flirted with me when he was nine! Neither does he immediately recognize me, now that I'm older. This day, he asked me if I had a phone book. I replied, "Yes I do." He said, "Let me see it." I pulled my phone book out and gave it to him. He writes his number in it and says, "Please use it!" Of course I never did, not yet anyway. He does call me once. After that call, he later told me he said to himself he would never call me again. I gave him that, "Oh it's you" attitude to blow him off. It's true about timing. It's everything, because five years later, I am sitting on my sofa looking through my phone book and this name and number jumps out at me. It was Ty's. I was curious to see if his number was the same. If it was, "What is he up to these days?" I thought. I called the number. It was around 8PM. "Hello", says a sleepy voice. "Ty, hi, it's Denise." He replied, "Who?" Ok, pay back for the, "Oh it's you" attitude when he called me five years earlier. I said, "You know, Denise, what's up? How are you?" In a tired voice he said, "I'm good, I was just sleeping. I just got off from work." At this point, Ty is working as a UPS driver. He tells me he is good and quickly lets me know he is a saved man now and not interested in no mess. I say, "That is good, because I am saved too and don't want no mess either." We talked a little more and he slowly warms up to me. I invite him over, but he is apprehensive and I say to him, "I won't bite!" He gets a chuckle out of that and the next day he comes up.

CHAPTER 22

OUR LIVES TRANSITION

I'm in the kitchen and there comes a knock at the door. "Come in!" I holler. In walks Ty. He is young (27 at that time), chocolaty skin, wavy hair, small waist, muscular thighs, which I saw because he had these tight shorts on with his UPS shirt on, sleeves rolled up showing his hard muscular arms. I am 36 at this point. Well, that was the beginning of the relationship that has turned into 24 years of marriage and counting. While at work at the Courthouse, with my co-worker who became my best friend, I was glowing about my new found love. When I explained who he was, my friend Doris, says, "Who? Young Ty??" My husband loves to play Tower of Power's, "You're Still a Young Man", because the song chronicles the plight of a young man such as he, attempting to win the love of an older lady. Each lyric of the song fits us to the "T".

We fell sexually a lot. We couldn't keep our hands off each other. Every time we sinned, Ty who was a street evangelist at that time and was already under early conviction by the word of God, would have us get on our knees to repent. About six weeks into the relationship, Ty asked me to marry him. Of course I said, "Yes!" He told me later that if I had said "No", he was prepared to move on because he couldn't continue to sin against God. After our divorces came through, we were married at the West Chester court house in Chester County, Pennsylvania by Judge Shenkin on March 18, 1991. Ty's mother surprised us. She was at the courthouse when we got there and witnessed our vows. I remember it was a cold, overcast, drizzly rainy day. It wasn't a planned day either. We got up, Ty said let's go do this; he called his mom to let her know we were getting married on that day and off we went. Our lives transitioned from courtship to family life.

Ty moved out from his apartment, into mine and then we moved again because with his income, our rent would have been more than if we lived in a regular apartment complex. One of my husband's beautiful qualities is he is honest and living the Word is as important as life itself. We were married two years and I didn't get pregnant. I really didn't want to have a baby because Joey was eight and I was used to the independence that came with him being older now. Ty didn't have any children, so for that reason I wanted to do it for him. I had gone to the doctor's and he ran a test which said that my tubes were blocked and I wouldn't be able to have a baby without surgery. I was concerned because our insurance wasn't going to cover this.

My husband prayed daily for me and over me. It wasn't until one day when I came home from work and fell on my knees and asked God to heal my womb and open my tubes. it wasn't until I came into agreement with my husband, that I became pregnant. Man (The doctor) said pregnancy was not possible without surgery. But God said, "Yes." Anything and everything is possible with God and agreement transacts the deal! My husband told me I was pregnant. He said the Lord showed the top of her head crowning, coming out of me in a vision, after we made love one night. He said the sight of this made him jump back, because he couldn't believe what he was seeing.

CHAPTER 23

APRIL 17, 1993

Ty bought a pregnancy test and sure enough I was pregnant. My pregnancy was considered high risk because I was now 39. I'm in my second trimester and the nurse wants to perform a procedure which penetrates the birth sac, for the purpose of drawing amniotic fluid, to see if the baby is free of complications. But also, the test itself can be very dangerous to the fetus. I let them know I didn't want it, nor did I need it, because my baby is fine. I had complete faith in God that he had me and my baby's well-being in his hands. When you operate in complete faith, God honors that thing you trust Him for and you know when you are operating in complete faith because you are free from worry and totally confident of a great outcome which is higher than man concerning that thing. My husband wanted a girl. On one of my visits for my check up, the nurse was rubbing the ultra sound wand all around my lubricated stomach and she says, "do you want to know what it is'? I say to her, "I already know, It's a girl." She says, "Yes you are right, how did you know?" I told her that a daughter is what we asked the Lord for. She smiled. The months rolled out without incident, with the exception of one thing, her name. My husband wanted to name her Shayla. I did not like that name and it was a little disturbing to me that I was going to have to live with my daughter's name being Shayla. But this shows how I am already in line submissively with my husband. I have learned the Lord will move according to my desire even if I disagree with my husband. But it starts with me and my submission to my husband. Well the Lord did NOT disappoint!

The Lord heard my heart cry because one night about 11pm, my husband woke up out of his sleep, lifted his head and said, "The Lord said, "Her name is Shayahna!" Thank you Jesus! I loved it! Don't tell me God doesn't care about the intimate details of our lives. In the weeks that followed my husband began to search for the meaning of her name. He found her name in a combination of Hebrew and Greek words, meaning, "Joy of God surely". I added her middle name, "Nicole", which comes from the Greek word *nike*, which means victory!

Shayahna arrived April 17, at 1:36 in the afternoon. Oh and guess what? It is my mom's birthday as well! What a joyous day! She was long, beautiful and she had a head full of sandy reddish brown hair. Her father held her first and he remarked that she had beautiful long fingers that she took and wrap around his finger tightly and today she still commands that same tight knit grip on her dad! "She is her father's daughter", I often say!

Ty, Joey and newborn baby Shayahna

This Is My Story

Me and Baby Shayahna

Me and my little girl

Me and the young woman Shayahna

This Is My Story

My Daughter, Shayahna

CHAPTER 24

MY CHILDREN

My children are grown now. I love them both. Often times when I think about them, my mind goes back to when they were young. I tried to be the best parent I could possibly be. Sometimes, I feel I didn't quite hit the mark with that. However, it certainly wasn't because of the lack of love. A solid foundation was put in place for both of them. The Word says; Train up a child in the way that he should go: and when he is old, he will not depart from it (Proverbs22:6).

My children, Joe and Shayahna

Each of us has been given free will. It was given by God. Sometimes our children cause us pain while they are trying to find their way. I penned this poem during one of those times;

This Is My Story

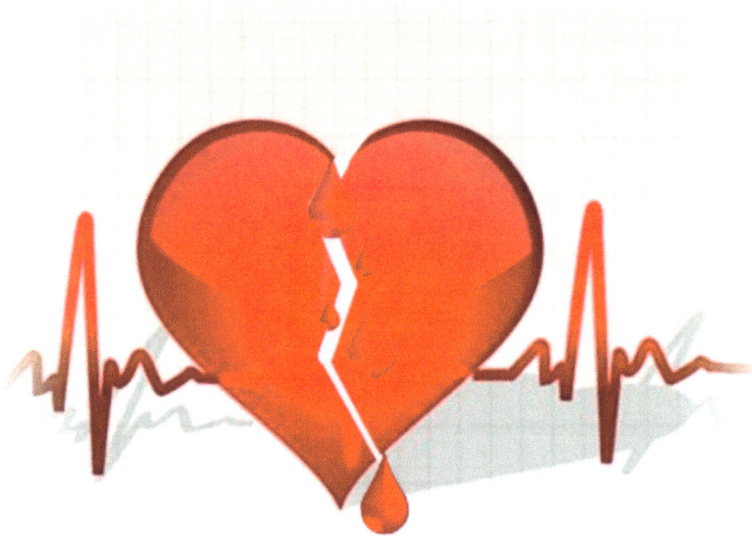

CHAPTER 25

A MOTHER'S CRYING HEART

All I can remember are days past that are quickly rushing to that point in eternity; days filled with sorrow, with a sprinkle of happiness and a serving of joy; a present filled with a past of longing; a heart broken by a child whom I only can glimpse in a fading memory. To put it frankly God, my mind is amazed at how my heart can go on beating under such a weight of sorrow. I love you. God loves you more. I can see how my love fades to a mere nothingness in comparison to His. It's a love unfeigned by sin; untainted by the harshness of this life; if you can't see my love, that's okay, but please look with your heart by faith and see God's love.

~Author~

Denise Y. Taylor-Smith

As the years rolled on there were more changes and new adjustments. There was moving from an apartment to a house and having my mother move in with us. There was a rebellious teenager, lots of arguing, moments of temptation in our marriage by both of us. James 1:15, Then when lust hath conceived, it bringeth forth sin: and sin, when it is finished, bringeth forth death. Well, we are blessed and honored that even though we have both been tempted, lust has not been transacted into adultery which may have brought about the death of our marriage. Our love has stood the test of temptation through time. It is stronger today than ever! Hallelujah!

My husband's mother died in 1999, then his father in 2001, 18 months later. They were married 48 years.

My In-laws, Linwood, Sr. and Isabel Smith

We moved again. This time, we purchased the house in which my husband was raised. I became a care giver for my mother. My mother goes into a nursing home for 2 years, where I continue to care for her and insure she is being taken care of. My mother passes in 2006 and then in 2010 my dad passes. I traveled to Boston by air, together with my sister Bernetta, to visit our dad in the hospital. He at this point is living in Boston. He is not conscious, but he knows we are there. We stayed a few days and he passed away a week after we had left. I did not fly back again to attend his funeral. During, my last visit with him, I spoke softly in his ear. I told him that I love him and I will see him in heaven. Even though he wasn't conscious I know he heard every word because a tear came from the corner of his eye and rolled down his cheek.

My husband and I, watching the mortality of our parents through death from this life and through the imperfections of their relationships, understand how truly blessed we are as a couple. The loss of our parents and the resulting pain of missing them has caused us to cleave together even more, because we understand all the more, the importance of commitment, sacrifice and love. Simply put, we are in love!!

Two turtle doves nested under our hedges last summer. We got such joy watching the pair! God's creation is awesome!

CHAPTER 26

MARRIAGE

Marriage is a gift from God. To keep the gift that keeps on giving, you must transact God's word concerning the marriage. I'm not a professional marriage counselor, but I can speak from the word of God and my own experience. At the head of our marriage is Christ, then my husband and then me. Why this order? Because God created all things. He created man. He used the dust of the earth to shape Adam and blew life into him. God saw Adam and declared that he should not be alone. So he put Adam into a deep sleep and took out a rib and created his woman, Eve. Man is to look after his wife and love her as Christ loves the church (Ephesians 5:25). Woman is supposed to see that she honors her husband in all things Ephesians 5:33b). This is not necessarily automatic, but it is the submission of will just like when you receive salvation. This is the word of God. The submission is the balanced answer to the husband's initiated unconditional love. If love and submission reign in your marriage anything can be overcome. Love will allow patience to have her perfect work. Forgiveness will be available in an abundant supply as you submit yourselves one to another in the fear of God (Ephesians 5:21). My husband has no space in which I am not welcomed. I have no space in which he is not welcomed. We are totally open and we share in every success and in every failure we find growth. What the enemy meant for evil, God uses it for our good. It is a beautiful thing to see or hear of a marriage that has lasted through the expanse of time, because you know it had to take a lot of love, and finesse to make that happen.

    My husband and I have been married for twenty four years, and counting. It has been twenty four years of fidelity, just by transacting the Word of God. Using the word of God, together with the Holy Spirit, anyone can transact fidelity to the glory of God. For men, don't let another woman's breast embrace your chest (Proverbs 5:20) and drink from your own cistern Proverbs 5:15-19. For Women use your arms of strength and gird your loins to back off any attempt by another man (Proverbs 31:17). Do not deny each other sex unless it is agreed upon by both parties for a time for the sake of prayer and fasting (I Corinthians 7:5). So ladies take "I have a headache" or "I'm too tired" off the marriage bed, not unless you are really sick. Also read I Corinthians 7:2-5 for more specific instruction. A wife is her husband's crown (Proverb 12:4). A Godly man living Kingdom principles, does not want a fake gold rhinestone encrusted crown upon his head.

Marriage is like a pot of well-put together soup. You need to add good quality ingredients; just the right amount of seasoning and allow it to simmer slowly for a while. Everyone who shares in it, feels the love it was made with and it warms the belly and touches the heart. But really, marriage is two people who are just sold out to each other, whether times are good or times are bad. When they are bad, just hold on. Don't give up! It will get back to the good if you love each other. Husbands don't be afraid to let your wife know that she means everything to you and that life just wouldn't be worth living if she weren't in it. Wives put away the bickering. Show and tell your husband you appreciate his every effort that he gives towards making the family whole. Wives be submissive to your husband. In fact, see to it that you honor him in all things great and small (Esther 1:20). Wives be strong, but, let your strength exude softness, gentleness, and kindness. When you come together at the end of the day, each of you should feel safe and loved and that together, there is nothing you can't overcome. Don't have secrets, hidden agendas or self-seeking motives. You should be able to lay bare before the one you have entrusted your life to. No one wants to be sleeping with the enemy. Now mind you all this doesn't just happen because you said, "I do." But you can never get to that sweet spot, if as soon trouble shows up, one of the parties quit. Oh and there is a sweet spot! In the vows, it says until death do we part, because it takes time to know all of what you have in each other, no matter if the time is short or long. Time is God given, so whatever it is, it is enough. Marriage requires imperfect people to work together towards perfecting the relationship. It is what you make it. People aren't perfect, but we do grow and mature and hopefully grow wiser through knowledge and learning from our mistakes. It's one thing to be knowledgeable. However, if that knowledge isn't applied to your living, you can't obtain wisdom.

The Bible says that the beginning of wisdom is the fear of the Lord. Anything that you want to last has to have a foundation that is true. That foundation has to be strong.

Life is heavy, so don't think for one minute you are going to be able to hold a marriage together with lust, vanity, selfishness, pride, fear, a lack of trust, dishonesty, unfaithfulness, unforgiveness and there is more, but you get the idea. A God ordained marriage is between a man and a woman. It is not open, but closed. When you come together the Bible says you are as one. If the marriage is open, you are one with many, so rather than a union, it is now a legion. I know someone might read this who is in opposition to some or everything I have said here. That is okay, for we all have a path to follow and a story to tell. I thank my Heavenly Father that I have chosen the narrow path.

Marriage or life can not be totally experienced with the mind, will or emotions. Yet, it is the combination of the three guided by the Spirit or spirits. As far as roles, it differs from family to family. You will find your comfort spot as you learn each other. Marriage is traditional in that it is between a man and a woman. After that, tradition goes out the window. If you are the woman in the marriage and you are the breadwinner, do not lord it over your husband. Let him be a man and lead the family. If God is at the head and the Holy Spirit abides, this is workable, for you should be operating as a unit. If you are Mr. Mom, make sure you are confident and strong and able to lead your family with love. When a woman looks after her household and cares for the children, this is valuable! It is no less valuable if the man does it.

Arguments are going to happen, but after the ranting and raving, come together with defenses down and talk about what caused you to argue. If you cannot resolve the problem in one talk, that's okay. But, at least confirm your love for each other and agree to work on it, whatever "it" may be. There is no room for pride in a marriage. This is all part of the good ingredients I talked about earlier.

Oh! That sweet spot I talked about, for me? It is when I think about my husband and I know I don't want to be anywhere in this world without him. You might speak your sweet spot a little differently, but ultimately it should take you back to your vows; for better or worse, for richer or poorer, till death do we part. My husband has no space that I am not welcome in and I have no space that he is not welcome in. We are totally open and we share in every success and every failure we grow from. What the enemy meant for evil, God uses it for our good.

CHAPTER 27

CRISIS AVERTED!

HIM -"You only love me to a point, after that you tell me to go pound sand! You are only in this marriage for convenience! I can't land because I don't trust you! Some time the love is on, sometimes it is off! I'm hurting and you kick me! You tell me if I'm not happy, go find another woman!

HER – You hurt me saying I only love you to a point. I've given you years of love, support and total fidelity. Yes, if we are arguing I say "fu", but that is because I am angry and frustrated because of the lack of words to express what I'm feeling. If you can't land that is not my fault! Why can't you trust me? I'm here, I'm with you. I'm not perfect, but I'm certainly not those things the devil attacks you with and says that I am.

STOP! Does any of this sound familiar? I hope not, but if so you can relate to our own little private hell, manufactured by the devil, based on taking advantage of each of our own insecurities. We all have them. Some of us are so good at keeping them covered, or masked, we don't even realize it ourselves, until that one thing hits, that makes you acknowledge it, in all of it's marriage, unraveling glory. When life is filled with working, and raising your children, taking care of aging parents, going back to school etc., a lot of stuff can fly under the radar. But when the time comes and it is just you and him, and him and you, that's when the real stuff comes to the surface. Time to retool and reintroduce so that you can get back to intimacy as quickly as possible!

CHAPTER 28

MARRIAGE HAS SEASONS

Marriage has seasons. The seasons can be good or bad. The bad seasons can be good and used as a point of personal growth and deeper intimacy for your marriage, if you are present. Present meaning you care and are willing. Even if you feel like love has left, it can be restored if both partners are willing to work things out. The fire of love has just died down a bit. Add some fuel and see what happens! Aside from the sex act itself, we find that just French kissing, embracing and looking into each others eyes keeps us settled and confirmed in our souls about our love for one another. Always stay on the same page with your mate. That doesn't mean you can't grow and change as a person, but bring all the positivity back to the marriage and share it. Don't let the enemy trick you into believing that you have outgrown your partner. Husbands give up that lie that she doesn't understand you! It's weak! She will understand you if you dare to really talk to her and allow her to listen to you, and listen to her as she talks to you. Wives, stop lying! Don't spend money that he doesn't know about. If he asked you not to use the credit card, don't use it. If you wreck the car, don't try to hide it and let him discover it on his own. This is all very deceptive and can be harmful to your spouse and devastating to your marriage. Jealousy is the rage of a man, the Bible says so. So if your husband thinks you're cheating for whatever reason and you are not, it will be pretty hard convincing him otherwise if you have lied in the past. Just like all sin is sin, so it is with lies. There is no such thing as a little white lie.

My husband is a man of determination, who is sincere. There is no pretense with him. He is honest, full of integrity and he is a man who strives for excellence and he is willing to go that extra mile to get the job done. Last, but certainly not least, he is a man of God which he attributes any good thing about himself is because of Him. Him being Jesus Christ.

All though my husband is well educated, there were some years, where opportunities were stolen from him as well as denied. It is hard for a Black man in America even a well-educated one. But, every tough place, every struggle, every position denied had something to offer. We grew stronger, we learned even better how to love our enemies and we learned that every **"No"** from man was a promotion from God and an opportunity to experience God's keeping as well as his promotion and preparation. I encouraged my husband to not return to teaching in 2012, but to step out by faith and start his own consulting business using the tools God gave him through education and his own natural God given talent. He did exactly that. ATS Consulting and Training, LLC; www.atsbusiness.com is the for-profit company, and The Coatesville Community Development Corporation, is the nonprofit company. My husband said he doesn't work for money, although we need money. But he works for impact and change according to his core purpose which comes from God. Money is a tool and the love of money is the root of every evil up to and including a race of people enslaving another race of people. It is not about skin color, but about controlling economics. Yet, through it all, my husband is known for the development of business, marketing and strategic plans that have helped to shape American business market spaces such as Wide Format print for pay in the successful Staples Wide Format Marketing Plan of 2003 to now. There are several community development plans gaining congressional and other high level leadership respect at the writing of this book by my husband and partners that have teamed up with him.

This Is My Story

The Lord sure has rewarded him in business as he was obedient to the charge. In the midst of all of this we started our ministry (Breakout Restoration Ministries) in 2000, where my husband is the pastor. Our motto is "Word, Worship and Service". We are a Full Gospel Church (meaning that if it is in the Word, we believe it! If it is not in the Word we don't bother with it! (I Corinthians 4). In church I sing along with my daughter and some support from my husband. We are worshipers. His preaching style is straight from the word of God, always bringing forth the praise and the glorification of our Lord. He is a keyboard player and music arranger. He also plays an Akai EWI which is an Electronic Wind Instrument (EWI) which uses saxophone fingering to play any number of synthesized sounds. He does it all for the glory of God!

King Twigg & the Royals

CHAPTER 29

THE CONVERSION OF KING TWIGG

My husband's musical inspiration comes from his father, a saxophonist and band leader. His father's band name was "King Twigg & the Royals". He played saxophone, keyboards and guitar. Ty, grew up hearing his father's band play all of the soul hits of the day, now classics. Songs from James Brown, Junior Walker and the Allstars, the Drifters, etc. Even though, neither Ty, nor his brother, Linwood Jr. chose music as a career, today, they both play wind instruments in their respective churches. The gift caught up to both of them later in life. We truly are another version of our parents! Aren't we?? What a blessing it is when the best traits of parents influence the lives of their children. My husband and his brother have played together in church and at the family reunion. We the family, know their dad would be so proud!

King Twigg's band at its peak in the early 1960's became a well sought after back-up band of the Jolly Joyce Agency in New York and Philadelphia. "Twigg" and his band, backed Little Anthony and the Imperials, Patti and the Blue Bells before she was simply, Patti Labelle and other national acts. My father-in-law played his instruments all the way until his last days. But he dropped, the "King" and only allowed others to call him, "Twigg". The reason? He had an experience in business in his later years of working that wasn't going so well. A very strong Christian brother led him to Christ and challenged my father-in-law to trust the Lord to bring him through. When the Lord did as the brother promised, my father-in-law's faith in Jesus Christ was clear until the day he passed away. The Lord can save at any age! He loved Dr. Fredrick KC Price's ministry. His testimony was, "Call me Twigg, Jesus is KING!"

CHAPTER 30

MY HUSBAND

My husband was working for UPS when we got together, at the end of the summer of 1990. He did have a Bachelor of Science in Industrial Arts Education Degree from Cheyney University, earned in 1984. He taught school for a year and then quit to work for Allstate Insurance as a claims adjuster. He kept his grocery store job at the same time. It was then, in 1985 that he attempted to date me to no avail. He left the 2 jobs to work for UPS which was a much better paying scenario. As stated before, 5 years later in 1990, we connected when I called him. So after we were together a while he left UPS and ended up teaching at Downingtown High School for 7 years. When we got together, we, my son and I went to his church where he was the audio sound guy. It was during this time that he heard the call of God calling him to minister. He said the Lord said to him he did not want another Master's of Divinity degree and that he had not exercised his talents in the earth. My husband was well versed in the word of God flap to flap taught and led by his Uncle, Rev. Clifford Hicks who is a conservative minister. My husband went back to secular graduate school following God's charge in 2002 at age 39. He would work all day in sales jobs with Xerox and a credit card processing company, leave work and go to school well into the evening, come home and eat, sleep a couple of hours and then get up and do school work and then shower and go right back out of the door to start all over again for five straight years. This was exhausting for him, it was exhausting for me. But man did it give him a mid-life professional boost!

But he kept up this charge until he accomplished what he set out to do. He earned a Master of Science in Information Science (Computer Engineering Degree) from Pennsylvania State University, a Master of Business Administration degree from University of Phoenix (Campus) and a Six Sigma certification from Villanova University. Six Sigma is a process that is used for project management and stats analysis for process improvement. This education coupled with his broad experiences working for companies as an employee and as a consultant, are the basis for our business consulting services to For-Profit, Non-Profit, municipal and Faith-based organizations.

My Husband and I

This Is My Story

CHAPTER 31

HOW WE KEEP OUR MARRIAGE SPICEY

SUB-CATEGORY

He is a romantic. After 24 years of marriage, he still strives to make love to my total being. We are still very much in young love. He says that he feels like he is just getting started with me. It causes me to feel like our marriage is continually refreshed and that he loves me and has not lost interest. I feel like I have not lost his attention. It truly makes me feel complete.

The card from flowers he sent me spontaneously when I worked at PNC Bank as a teller.

The card says, "My heart beats in unison with yours."

I Love You, Ty

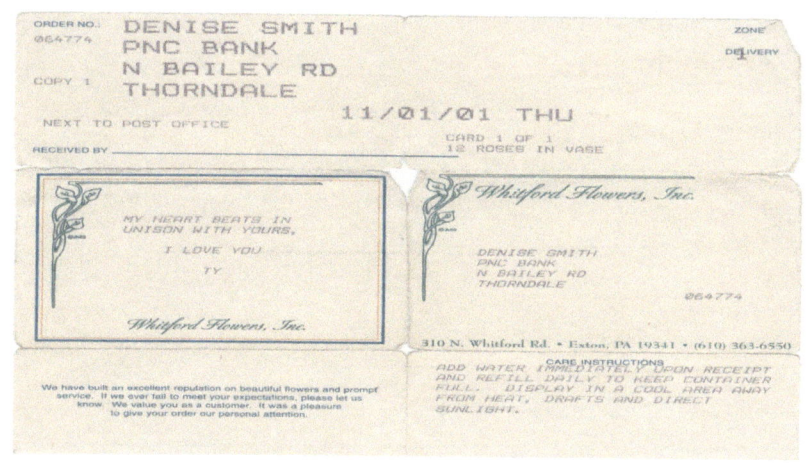

The Bible says that marriage is honorable in all and the marriage bed is undefiled (Hebrews 13:4). It also says he that is set free is free indeed (John 8:33). We try different things to add spice to our sex life. However, it does not include the addition of other partners! Sexy lingerie does not violate scripture. The Song of Solomon describes what my husband captures on his digital camera! My husband and I keep it spicy. I'm his model and his every fantasy. You too can explore what keeps the fire burning in your marriage. So here is one of those categories I spoke about earlier on. I'm a lingerie model for my husband only. I model for my husband beautiful lingerie that he buys for me. He's happy and I'm happy to do it. I'm smiling right now. So explore with your spouse and find your own spice. Your husband will be happy, you will be happy and God will be pleased. Appropriate passion is like owning your own deep well filled with fresh, cool spring water waiting for you to drop your bucket and pull up and take a nice long refreshing drink! "Stay thirsty my friends" for each other! God will hold back no good thing! These pictures are not meant to offend, but to show that sexual beauty is not dirty. It is not my intent to produce lust in anyone. I only wish to encourage sexier, stronger, healthier, loving relationships! A woman can capture sexiness for her husband at virtually any age.

"Pro 5:19 [Let her breast] the loving hind and pleasant roe; let her breasts satisfy thee at all times; and be thou ravished always with her love."

This Is My Story

This Is My Story

This Is My Story

CHAPTER 32

LIVE YOUR DAYS INSPIRED ANEW

Every day that we live is an opportunity to do something positive. Just think that one something or anything, can be a building block for something great. No one builds the whole ship by himself. But, you do hold a crucial piece that will allow that ship to someday set sail. Don't be selfish! Don't be fearful! Don't be lazy! Your piece is important! You fit in! You count! When the ship is christened and launched we all move forward. When we say or do something to help someone else in the most positive way, then our living will not be in vain.

I love Lydia Tillman's story of triumphant over her adversity and the saying she attached to it, "Live Your Days Inspired Anew", because like Lydia, I and you; have our own adversity to overcome.

If we adopt a Kingdom mentality according to the Eternal Purpose of God and from the vantage of the sheer fact that He IS without respect to time. Remember that He is ever present, bounding beyond all time past through eternity past. He is ever present, bounding beyond all time future through eternity future! We have eternity in our spirit and our soul (If the soul is born again). So we have the ability to sit with Him in heavenly places (Ephesians 2:6). We can experience the fullness of God that passes our knowledge and is guaranteed because He loves us (Ephesians 3:19). Since that fullness is dependent on us knowing His love? Than grasp that the strengthening that you have received is proof and fact that you KNOW that you are loved! And to know that you are loved brings contentment.

The miraculous is only miraculous because we don't believe, but, when we believe all things are possible. Believe that in every case that He loves you and you will experience His fullness. And with His fullness comes exceeding, great power that works in and through you! (Ephesians 3:20)

CHAPTER 33

PRAISE OF A VIRTUOUS WOMAN
Proverbs 31

10; Who can find a virtuous woman? For her price is far above rubies. 11; The heart of her husband doth safely trust in her, so that he shall have no need of spoil. 12; She will do him good and not evil all the days of her life. 17; She girdeth her loins with strength, and strengtheneth her arms 23; Her husband is known in the gates, when he sitteth among the elders of the land. 25; Strength and honor are her clothing; and she shall rejoice in time to come. She openeth her mouth with wisdom; and in her tongue is the law of kindness. 23; Her children arise up, and call her blessed; her husband also, and he praiseth her. 30; Favor is deceitful, and beauty is vain: but a woman that feareth the Lord, she shall be praised.

So, who am I? I am a woman who has embodied a little girl who was deeply hurt by those she should have been able to trust and protected thereby. I became a teenager and then a young woman using my body and beauty as a bargaining chip for love. Then one day I was awaken to the fact that I already possessed the greatest love of all. By receiving and possessing this love I found I was able to trust, hope, believe, expect and receive my heart's desire to the fullness of the stature of Christ! And to the overflow by the Father! Often times what one really desires aren't things that can be seen or held, but the things that empower your soul to soar to heights that shock even yourself. That's how amazingly His love transforms! In a world where women clothed themselves with fake, hype, hysteria and independence, I find myself clothed by my Creator in love, peace, righteousness, holiness and marriage. We are truly one flesh and Christ is the head. A threefold cord is not easily broken and my husband sits in the gates and...

I AM A VIRTUOUS WOMAN!

ACKNOWLEDGEMENTS

To my son, I once loved your dad. That part of my life was just as valid as the rest of it because it produced you, my son. You have many more things to accomplish according to what God has placed in your heart. Your best days are yet to come! God filled and ordained! Get positioned, stay positioned and your purpose will overtake you. Thank you for our beautiful grandchildren! Each one is beautiful and God given. I love them and I love you!

To my Daughter, you are beautiful, smart, kind, talented and genuine. Stay on the narrow road for the purpose God has placed in you. Thank you for growing up and watching out for your Dad and I!! And gurl you can sang!!! I love you!

To my sister Bernetta, due to life's circumstances we have missed so much together as sisters, but my prayer is that we can come together more, with love, understanding and patience for one another. I love you, I'm glad you are my sister and I am glad you and Jimmy found each other.

To my sister Char-lee, I remember when you were about 1 year old and I held you in my arms while you slept. I remember wanting it to be that way always. I love you!

Judy, thank you for allowing the Lord to use you to wake me up! You shared your piece and that jumped it off for me! I hope all is well with you and your family. Even though we have not kept in touch, our friendship is forever! Much love to you!

ACKNOWLEDGEMENTS

Doris, what can I say, but you are my friend. We may not talk or see each other everyday, but when we do, it's like we were never apart. Our comfortably level is that of loving sisters. Love you girl!

Christine, I love how you are able to stay so even natured even when going through tough times and you are able to keep such a positive attitude in the face of ugliness. You are my friend and I love you.

Prophetess Hope Bell you prophesied to me and said, "There is a book in there". You are a mighty woman of God, you are my friend.

ACKNOWLEDGEMENTS

To my husband, I love you more today than from when we first started out. You are the love and lover of my life and you play my heart like a sweet melody. You are my best friend. Truly our love is like fine wine that just keeps getting better with time. I'm so thankful that we have hung in there together when the bad times seemed like it would take us out. You have loved me, you have cared for me, you have taught me many, many things; scripturally and just good common sense for living. I love your ounce of prevention is worth more than a pound of cure approach. You are wise, strong and so, so kind, and so often misunderstood. I love how you always can have a smile and how you love all people especially the down trodden, women and children. You are my protector and defender, my Boaz. Above all, you attribute nothing to yourself but only to Christ. Truly you are my gift from God. When I see you, I can truly say that the Lord heard my cry.

I love you Honey!

Thank you Jesus!

DEDICATIONS

In loving memory of my Mother and Father, I know both of your souls are resting in peace. In spite of the dysfunction and adversity that was in our home, you did provide a foundation of wealth through faith in Jesus Christ! Because of that alone I am wealthier than the richest person on this planet. For that I am grateful!

In loving memory of my Grandma Florence, you were always there for me. I love you and still miss you.

In loving memory of my Grandma Pauline, as a child growing up you never missed my birthdays, you always wrote me letters and your love for me was unmistakable. Now that I am a grandmother I can appreciate that effort you put into making sure I knew I was loved even though we weren't always close in proximity. I love you and miss you.

In loving memory of my sister Dedra Pauline Taylor and my brother Kimberly Johnathan Taylor, I'll see you in Heaven when I get there.

More Words From The Author

We all can agree, this life is temporary. Why wouldn't we do our due diligence to secure our souls through the finished work of the cross by faith, and the souls of all who will. The work has been done. It is just a decision on our part. My prayer is that everyone who takes the time to read my book will allow Jesus to deal with their issues so that their faith will be complete and their purpose be fulfilled. May you prosper as your soul prospers!

Psalm 34:1

I will bless the Lord at all times: his praise shall continually be in my mouth

Hebrews 13: 15,16

By him therefore let us offer the sacrifice of praise to God continually, that is the fruit of our lips giving thanks to his name. But to do good and to communicate forget not for with such sacrifices God is well pleased.

www.ingramcontent.com/pod-product-compliance
Lightning Source LLC
Chambersburg PA
CBHW041432300426
44117CB00001B/8